FOR THE BEST DAD EVER

FOR THE BEST DAD EVER

This edition copyright © Octopus Publishing Group Limited, 2026
First published in 2020

All rights reserved.

No part of this book may be reproduced by any means, nor transmitted, nor translated into a machine language, without the written permission of the publishers.

Condition of Sale
This book is sold subject to the condition that it shall not, by way of trade or otherwise, be lent, resold, hired out or otherwise circulated in any form of binding or cover other than that in which it is published and without a similar condition including this condition being imposed on the subsequent purchaser.

An Hachette UK Company
www.hachette.co.uk

Summersdale Publishers
Part of Octopus Publishing Group Limited
Carmelite House
50 Victoria Embankment
LONDON
EC4Y 0DZ
UK

This FSC® label means that materials and other controlled sources used for the product have been responsibly sourced

www.summersdale.com

The authorized representative in the EEA is Hachette Ireland, 8 Castlecourt Centre, Dublin 15, D15 XTP3, Ireland (email: info@hbgi.ie)

Printed and bound in China

ISBN: 978-1-83799-769-5
eISBN: 978-1-83799-770-1

Substantial discounts on bulk quantities of Summersdale books are available to corporations, professional associations and other organizations. For details contact general enquiries: telephone: +44 (0) 1243 771107 or email: enquiries@summersdale.com.

To......................

From..................

> FATHERING IS NOT SOMETHING PERFECT MEN DO, BUT SOMETHING THAT PERFECTS THE MAN.
>
> **Frank Pittman**

> MY DAD BELIEVED IN ME, EVEN WHEN I DIDN'T.
>
> TAYLOR SWIFT

> My dad has given me the best gift anyone has ever given me. He gave me wings to fly.

ADRIA ARJONA

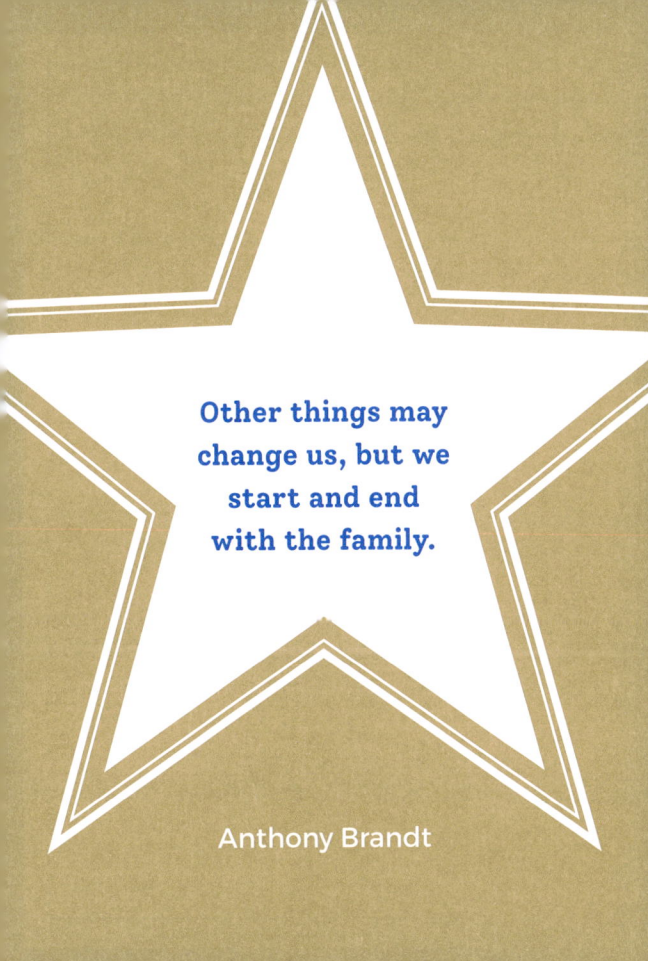

My daddy was my hero – he was always there for me when I needed him.

BINDI IRWIN

I've jumped out of helicopters… and played baseball in a professional stadium, but none of it means anything compared to being somebody's daddy.

CHRIS PRATT

> MY FATHER WAS MY TEACHER. BUT MOST IMPORTANTLY HE WAS A GREAT DAD.

Beau Bridges

I feel bad for other people... I clearly got the best dad!

You can tell what was the best year of your father's life, because they seem to freeze that clothing style and ride it out.

JERRY SEINFELD

> Never is a man more of a man than when he is the father of a newborn.
>
> — Matthew McConaughey

Govern a family as you would cook a small fish – very gently.

CHINESE PROVERB

A FATHER IS A GIANT FROM WHOSE SHOULDERS YOU CAN SEE FOREVER.

Perry Garfinkel

> **Dad taught me everything I know. Unfortunately, he didn't teach me everything he knows.**
>
> **AL UNSER JR**

I love my father as the stars – he's a bright shining example and a happy twinkling in my heart.

TERRI GUILLEMETS

DAD IS JUST ANOTHER WORD FOR HOME

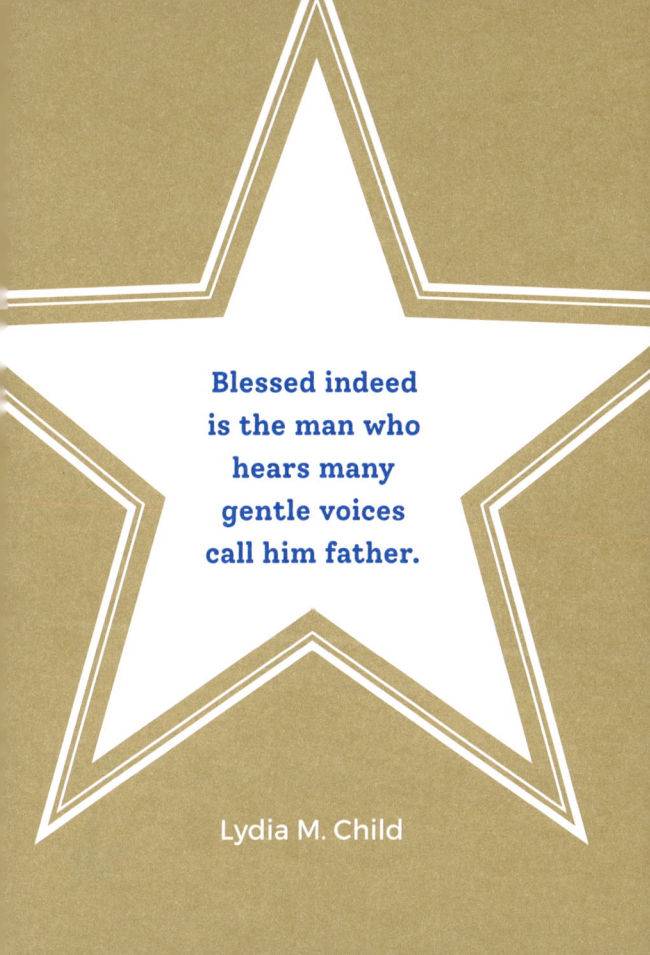

I was selfish before. Everyone is. But when you have kids, they become your main priority.

DAVID BECKHAM

JUST TAUGHT MY

KIDS ABOUT TAXES BY

EATING 38 PER CENT

OF THEIR ICE CREAM.

Conan O'Brien

IT'S THE COURAGE TO RAISE A CHILD THAT MAKES YOU A FATHER.

BARACK OBAMA

Being a great father is like shaving. No matter how good you shaved today, you have to do it again tomorrow.

REED B. MARKHAM

THERE'S NO PILLOW QUITE SO SOFT AS A FATHER'S STRONG SHOULDER.

Richard L. Evans

Raising kids is part joy and part guerrilla warfare.

ED ASNER

My father didn't tell me how to live; he lived, and let me watch him do it.

CLARENCE BUDINGTON KELLAND

DAD TO THE RESCUE!

When I was a kid, I used to imagine animals running under my bed. I told my dad... He cut the legs off the bed.

LOU BROCK

Of all the titles
I've been privileged
to have, "Dad" has
always been
the best.

Ken Norton

I WOULD WANT MY LEGACY TO BE THAT I WAS A GREAT SON, FATHER AND FRIEND.

Dante Hall

Character is largely caught, and the father and the home should be the great sources of character infection.

FRANK H. CHELEY

Dads are most ordinary men turned by love into heroes, adventurers, storytellers, and singers of song.

PAM BROWN

It's only when you grow up
and step back from him...
it's only then that you can
measure his greatness
and fully appreciate it.

MARGARET TRUMAN ON FATHERS

Everything I am, you helped me to be

Dads are stone skimmers, mud wallowers, water wallopers, ceiling swoopers, shoulder gallopers, upsy-downsy, over-and-through, round-and-about whooshers.

HELEN THOMSON

I am not ashamed to say that no man I ever met was my father's equal, and I never loved any other man as much.

HEDY LAMARR

IT'S BEEN THE MOST AMAZING EXPERIENCE I COULD EVER POSSIBLY IMAGINE.

Prince Harry, Duke of Sussex
on becoming a dad

[My dad] never stopped working to make sure we had the best life possible.

Chrissy Teigen

It is amazing how quickly the kids learn to drive a car, yet are unable to understand the lawnmower... or vacuum cleaner.

BEN BERGER

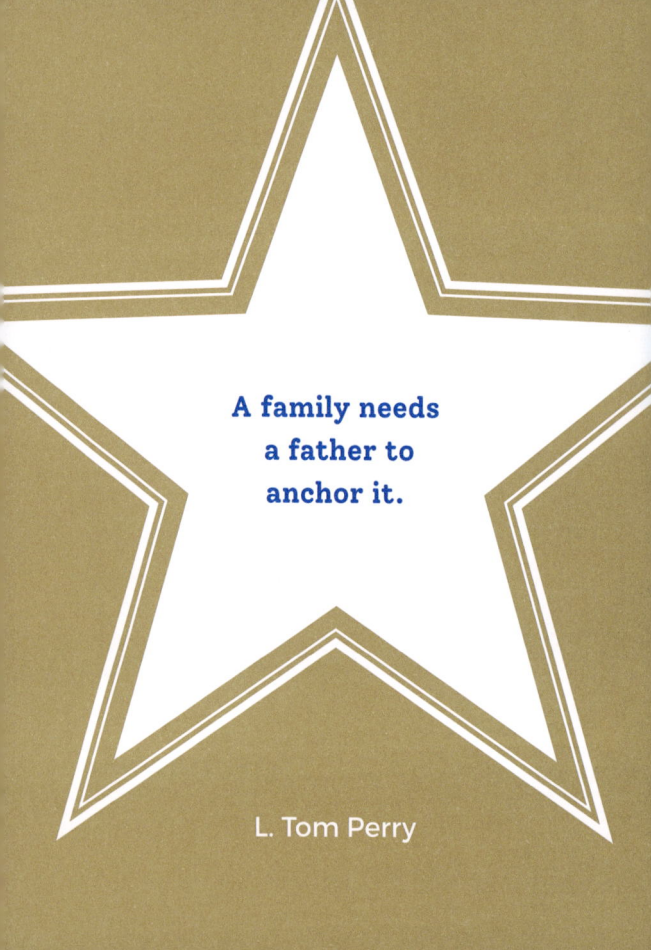

An almost perfect relationship with his father was the earthly root of all his wisdom.

C. S. LEWIS

YOU INSPIRE ME TO WORK HARD AND FOLLOW MY DREAMS

I'M LOOKING AT [MY DAUGHTER] RIGHT NOW. TO THINK THAT I AM HER DAD IS THE GREATEST HONOUR IN THE WORLD.

Harry Connick Jr

Start children off on the way they should go, and even when they are old they will not turn from it.

PROVERBS 22:6

IT IS A WISE FATHER THAT KNOWS HIS OWN CHILD.

WILLIAM SHAKESPEARE

I believe that what we become depends on what our fathers teach us... We are formed by little scraps of wisdom.

UMBERTO ECO

> We looked up
> to our father.
> He still is much
> greater than us.

Wynton Marsalis

> **You don't raise heroes, you raise sons. And if you treat them like sons, they'll turn out to be heroes.**
>
> **WALTER M. SCHIRRA SR**

I AM SO GRATEFUL FOR ALL YOU'VE DONE FOR ME

THE SOONER YOU TREAT YOUR SON AS A MAN, THE SOONER HE WILL BE ONE.

John Dryden

Each day of our lives we make deposits in the memory banks of our children.

CHARLES R. SWINDOLL

BEING A FATHER IS THE SINGLE GREATEST FEELING ON EARTH.

RYAN REYNOLDS

> My dad. One of the wisest, most authentic, integrity filled, heartful people I've ever known. He shaped me into who I am.

CONNIE BRITTON

A father is someone you look up to no matter how tall you grow.

Anonymous

THERE'S NOTHING THAT MAKES YOU MORE INSANE THAN FAMILY. OR MORE HAPPY.

Jim Butcher

I am a better person because of you

THE RAISING OF A CHILD IS THE BUILDING OF A CATHEDRAL. YOU CAN'T CUT CORNERS.

Dave Eggers

Anyone who tells you fatherhood is the greatest thing that can happen to you, they are understating it.

MIKE MYERS

Being a father has been, without a doubt, my greatest source of achievement, pride and inspiration.

NAVEEN JAIN

BEING A FATHER, BEING A FRIEND, THOSE ARE THE THINGS THAT MAKE ME FEEL SUCCESSFUL.

William Hurt

> **OLD AS SHE WAS, SHE STILL MISSED HER DADDY SOMETIMES.**
>
> GLORIA NAYLOR

Father, Dad, Papa, no matter what you call them they influence our lives and they are the person we look up to.

CATHERINE PULSIFER

I AM PROUD TO CALL YOU MY DAD

My father, he was like the rock, the guy you went to with every problem.

Gwyneth Paltrow

WHEN MY FATHER DIDN'T HAVE MY HAND, HE HAD MY BACK.

Linda Poindexter

Having children is like living in a frat house. Nobody sleeps, everything's broken, and there's a lot of throwing up.

RAY ROMANO

By the time a man realizes that maybe his father was right, he usually has a son who thinks he's wrong.

CHARLES WADSWORTH

My father gave me the greatest gift anyone could give another person.
He believed in me.

JIM VALVANO

Children have never been very good at listening to their elders, but they have never failed to imitate them.

JAMES BALDWIN

A FATHER IS MORE LIKELY TO FEED TEN CHILDREN THAN TEN CHILDREN ONE FATHER.

German proverb

A father's solemn duty is to watch football with his children and teach them when to shout at the ref.

PAUL COLLINS

Always kiss your children goodnight, even if they're already asleep.

H. Jackson Brown Jr

> IT IS NOT FLESH AND BLOOD, BUT THE HEART WHICH MAKES US FATHERS AND SONS.
>
> Johann Friedrich von Schiller

YOU'RE MORE THAN MY FATHER – YOU'RE MY FRIEND

Sometimes the poorest man leaves his children the richest inheritance.

RUTH E. RENKEL

IF YOUR CHILDREN LOOK UP TO YOU, YOU'VE MADE A SUCCESS OF LIFE'S BIGGEST JOB.

ANONYMOUS

It has given me purpose, taught me patience, and expanded my heart.

NEIL PATRICK HARRIS

ON FATHERHOOD

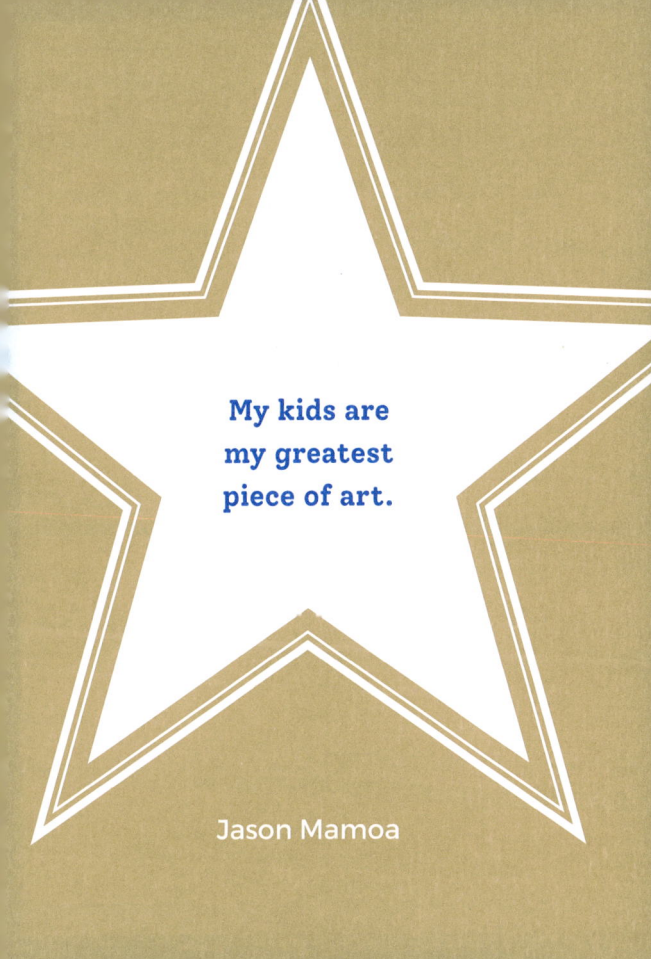

YOU KNOW ME BETTER THAN ANYONE

My mother gave me my drive, but my father gave me my dreams.

LIZA MINNELLI

There's no one
I'd rather be
with than
my kids.

Ralph Lauren

I CANNOT THINK OF ANY NEED IN CHILDHOOD AS STRONG AS THE NEED FOR A FATHER'S PROTECTION.

SIGMUND FREUD

YOU WILL ALWAYS BE YOUR CHILD'S FAVOURITE TOY.

VICKI LANSKY

My dad is truly the best. He is everything a father should be and the greatest man I will ever know.

DAKOTA FANNING

MEN GROW INTO FATHERS AND FATHERING IS A VERY IMPORTANT STAGE IN THEIR DEVELOPMENT.

David Gottesman

[Dad] opened the jar of pickles when no one else could.

Erma Bombeck

FAMILY IS NOT AN IMPORTANT THING. IT'S EVERYTHING.

Michael J. Fox

THE SECRET OF FATHERHOOD IS KNOWING WHEN TO STOP TICKLING.

ANONYMOUS

I don't tell you enough, but you mean so much to me

> **Father! – to God himself we cannot give a holier name.**

WILLIAM WORDSWORTH

Your children need
your presence more
than your presents.

JESSE JACKSON

There's nothing more contagious than the dignity of a father.

Amit Ray

> I haven't taught people
> in 50 years what
> my father taught by
> example in one week.

MARIO CUOMO

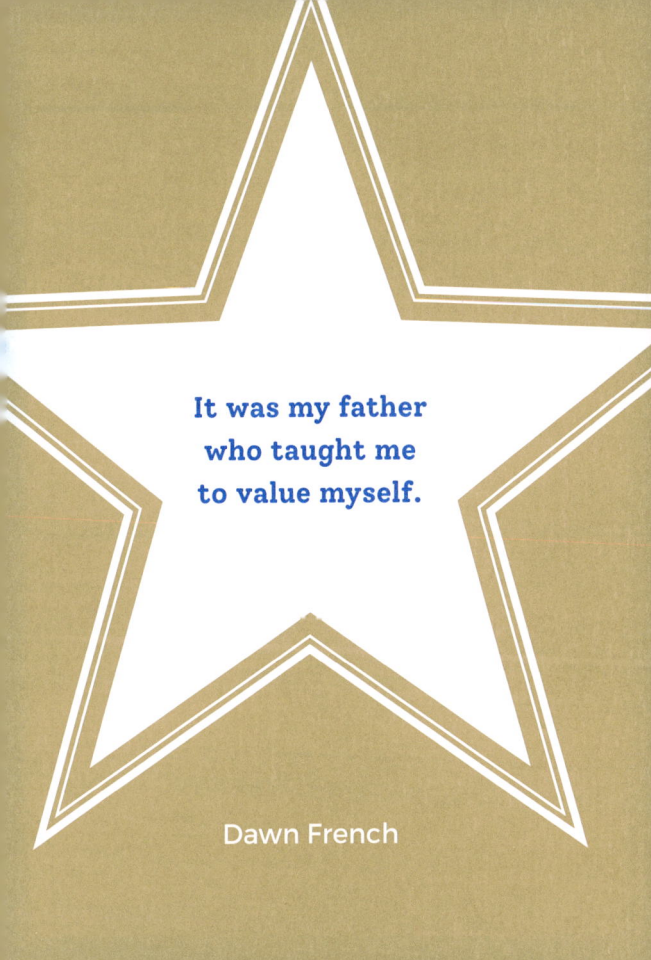

YOU'RE ALWAYS AROUND WHEN I NEED YOU

Be kind to thy father, for when thou wert young, who loved thee so fondly as he?

MARGARET ANN COURTNEY

MY DAD'S PANTS KEPT CREEPING UP ON HIM. BY 65 HE WAS JUST A PAIR OF PANTS AND A HEAD.

Jeff Altman

> Most of the time, I feel entirely unqualified to be a parent. I call these times being awake.
>
> **JIM GAFFIGAN**

A lot of my strength
comes from my dad.

TANYA TUCKER

[My father] was very important to me, because he made me think.

Janis Joplin

My kids are my number one priority no matter what I'm doing.

LIN-MANUEL MIRANDA

FATHER OF FATHERS,

MAKE ME ONE,

A FIT EXAMPLE

FOR A SON.

Douglas Malloch

I smile because you're my father; I laugh because there's nothing you can do about it

LIFE DOESN'T COME WITH AN INSTRUCTION BOOK; THAT'S WHY WE HAVE FATHERS.

H. JACKSON BROWN JR

There is a special place in
heaven for the father who
takes his daughter shopping.

JOHN SINOR

I DON'T MIND LOOKING IN THE MIRROR AND SEEING MY FATHER.

Michael Douglas

> **If you ever want to torture my dad, tie him up and right in front of him, refold a map incorrectly.**
>
> **CATHY LADMAN**

Families are the compass that guides us.

Brad Henry

I've never slept less and dealt with more poop and been so excited about it!

JUSTIN TIMBERLAKE ON BECOMING A DAD

THERE'S NOTHING LIKE AN ADVENTURE WITH DAD

HAVING ONE CHILD MAKES YOU A PARENT; HAVING TWO, YOU ARE A REFEREE.

David Frost

THERE IS NO JOB MORE IMPORTANT THAN PARENTING.

BEN CARSON

> He was a father.
> That's what a father
> does. Eases the burdens
> of those he loves.

GEORGE SAUNDERS

Setting a good example
for your children
takes all the fun out
of middle age.

WILLIAM FEATHER

> As I've gotten older,
> I've realized my true
> models are my parents...
> My dad is so strong.

ZENDAYA

MY DAUGHTER GOT ME A "WORLD'S BEST DAD" MUG. SO WE KNOW SHE'S SARCASTIC.

Bob Odenkirk

IF AT FIRST YOU DON'T SUCCEED, CALL DAD!

When I was twenty-something, I asked my father, "When did you start feeling like a grown-up?" His response: "Never."

SHANNON CELEBI

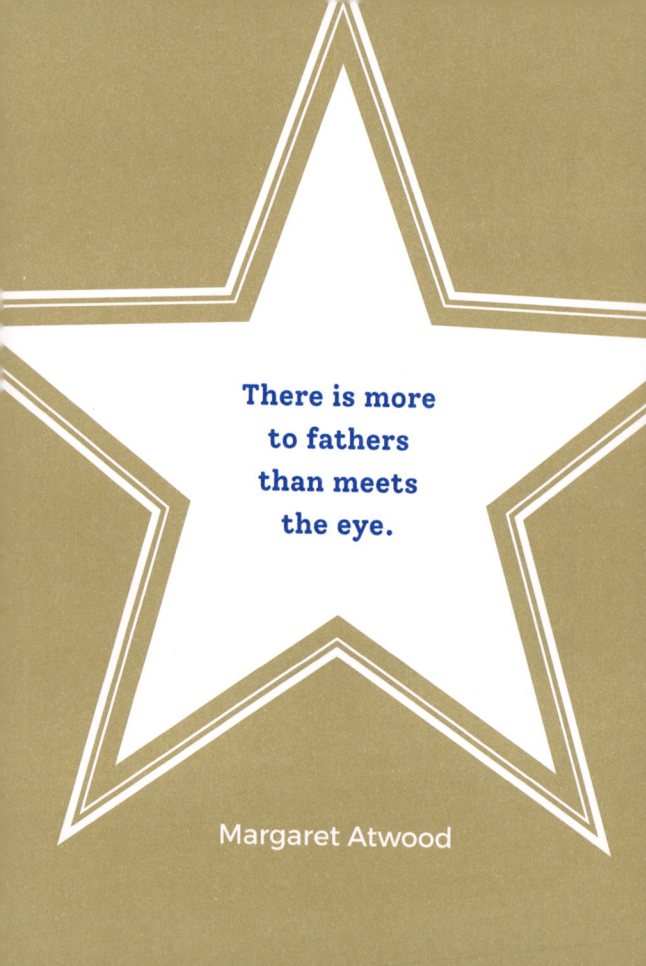

> IT ISN'T THE SIZE OF THE FAMILY, IT'S THE INTERACTIONS OF THE MEMBERS INSIDE.
>
> — MICHELE BORBA

A father's
smile has been
known to light
up a child's
entire day.

Susan Gale

Success, and even life itself, wouldn't be worth anything if I didn't have my children by my side.

CHILDREN LEARN TO SMILE FROM THEIR PARENTS.

SHINICHI SUZUKI

My father is my rock. It's where I learned everything about loyalty, dependability, being there day in, day out, no matter what.

HUGH JACKMAN

I will never grow too old for a hug

> **I realized being a father is the greatest job I have ever had and the greatest job I will ever have.**
>
> **DWAYNE JOHNSON**

THE HEART OF A FATHER

IS A MASTERPIECE

OF NATURE.

Antoine François
Prévost d'Exiles

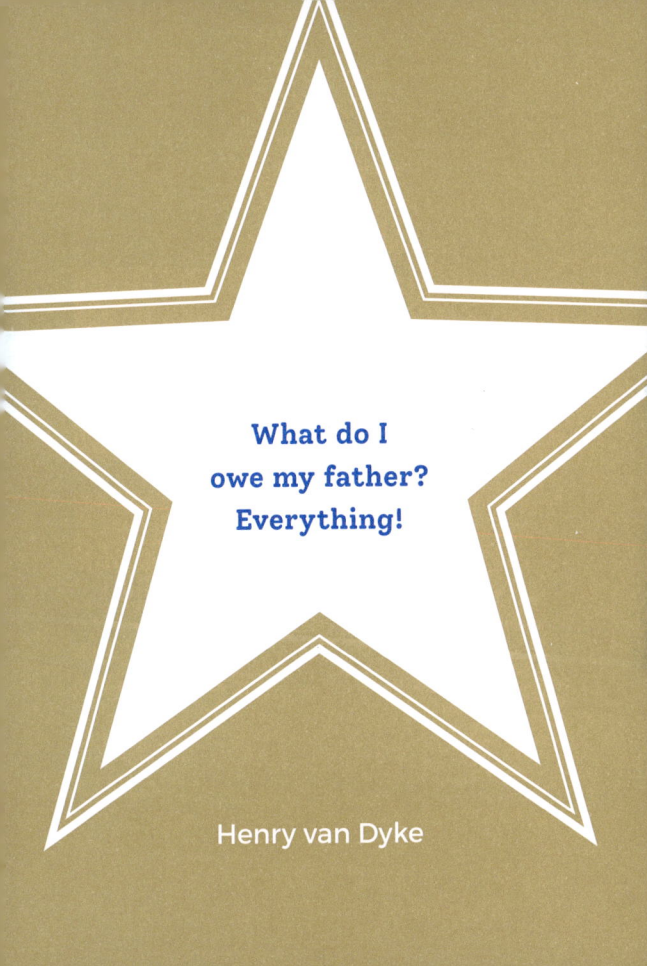

LATELY, ALL MY FRIENDS ARE WORRIED THAT THEY'RE TURNING INTO THEIR FATHERS. I'M WORRIED THAT I'M NOT.

Dan Zevin

Confident women
are raised by
loving dads.

Nitya Prakash

I EVEN LAUGH AT YOUR DAD JOKES

> **I'm looking out for myself, but I'm looking out for my dad, too.**
>
> **JAMIE REDKNAPP**

A daughter needs a dad
to be the standard against
which she will judge all men.

GREGORY E. LANG

A FATHER IS A BANKER

PROVIDED BY NATURE.

French proverb

> Nothing could get at me if I curled up on my father's lap... All about him was safe.

Naomi Mitchison

> I have found the best way to give advice to your children is to find out what they want and then advise them to do it.

HARRY S. TRUMAN

FATHERHOOD IS THE GREATEST THING THAT COULD EVER HAPPEN.

MICHAEL BUBLÉ

[My child] gave me the
reason to be a better
man and father.

COLIN FARRELL

THE MOST IMPORTANT THING IN THE WORLD IS FAMILY AND LOVE.

John Wooden

My dad is a hero. I'm never free of a problem, nor do I truly experience joy until we share it.

NANCY SINATRA

Having a kid is like falling in love for the first time when you're 12, but every day.

MIKE MYERS

Your father is your shelter.

Anonymous

A father is a man
who expects his son
to be as good a man
as he meant to be.

FRANK A. CLARK

ONE FATHER IS MORE THAN A HUNDRED SCHOOLMASTERS.

George Herbert

YOU'RE TOTALLY RAD, DAD

Every son's first superhero is his father, and it was the same for me. For me, he was Superman and Batman combined.

TIGER SHROFF

**DAD HUGS
ARE THE
BEST HUGS**

> **OF ALL THE ROCKS UPON WHICH WE BUILD OUR LIVES... FAMILY IS THE MOST IMPORTANT.**
>
> Barack Obama

A child looks up at the stars and wonders. A great father puts a child on his shoulders and helps them to grab a star.

REED B. MARKHAM

PARENTHOOD REMAINS THE GREATEST SINGLE PRESERVE OF THE AMATEUR.

ALVIN TOFFLER

A FATHER IS THE ONE FRIEND UPON WHOM WE CAN ALWAYS RELY.

Émile Gaboriau